farnham **maltings**

T0313553

The Band Back Together

By Barney Norris

Fri 08 March–Sun 14 April 2024

The Band Back Together was first performed at Farnham Maltings
on Fri 08 March 2024

The Band Back Together
by Barney Norris

Original Cast

Joe   **James Westphal**

Ellie   **Laura Evelyn**

Ross   **Royce Cronin**

Creative Team

Writer and Director   **Barney Norris**

Designer   **Becci Kenning**

Musical Director   **Tom Cook**

Lighting Consultant   **Joshua Sanderson**

Company Stage Manager   **Vicki Cox**

Foreword

I first started writing *The Band Back Together* two years ago, when Farnham Maltings approached me with the idea of writing a story for them. Their producer, Katy Potter, knew I'd grown up in Salisbury, and thought it would be excellent to write something about that city in the wake of Novichok. That chemical attack on UK soil was a profound tragedy for the city I come from. The unrest visited on the area was well documented in the TV drama, *The Salisbury Poisonings*, but I felt there was still more to say. I'd written about Salisbury throughout my career, particularly in my novel *Five Rivers Met on a Wooded Plain*, and I'd always thought the place was interesting because it was a kind of oxbow lake: away from the centre, therefore filled with curiosities. When the Novichok events occurred, I saw my city in a different light – what was being attacked wasn't a forgotten corner of England, but its heart: the place we see on shortbread tins, an idyllic, idealised version of our country. What was attacked was the English dreaming. I was excited to spend some time thinking about that, to reinterrogate the meaning of my city in the light of what had happened.

I first started writing *The Band Back Together* ten years ago, when Farnham Maltings got in touch out of the blue to say they'd seen a play of mine, and would like to meet to talk about work. I travelled out to Farnham – actually the first time I caught the wrong train and went to Petersfield, so the meeting had to be rescheduled, but in the end I got there and met the then artistic director. We created a touring show together called *While We're Here*, about homelessness and loneliness in Havant (I pick all the fun subjects), which opened the Bush Theatre's new studio and ended up on BBC Radio 4. I became an associate of the Maltings, and they told me they'd like to commission another play from me. We talked for a long time about what that might be. Then five summers after making *While We're Here*, I was invited on an artist's retreat where I met Katy and her colleagues Will Arnold and Eloise Talbot-Hammond, and we got talking, and the idea for a play finally started to emerge.

I first started writing *The Band Back Together* twenty-seven years ago, when I moved to Salisbury and latched onto that place as important to me, a place that somehow expressed my life. I grew up in that city, and loved it very much, but had to leave after school because I couldn't have the career I wanted there. I never stopped thinking about it, caring about it, writing about it – the things I wrote became my career, became my life. I carried Salisbury with me, I suppose. At thirty-six, twice the age I had been when I last lived there, I saved up the money for a one-bed flat and moved home to be part of my city again. I'd been living in Farnham till shortly before, in Upper Hale; perhaps I'll write that play next, if the Maltings will have me back again.

Returning to Salisbury brought me strongly into contact with how my life had gone, and my own mortality. I thought about how much the place had changed, and how I'd changed. I wandered round the city with old friends, collecting material for a story about who I'd thought I was going to be, and who I'd actually become, and the things that had happened which separated those two people. And a story, above all, about the things I still loved – my city, my friends, and the dreams which formed me as a teenager, which still guide my life today. *The Band Back Together* was the product of that – a love story about a place, and lost time, and old friends, and dreams that didn't happen.

Barney Norris
February 2024

Original Cast

Laura Evelyn | Ellie

Laura is an actor, writer and improviser based in London.

Theatre credits include: *Red Ellen* (UK tour for Northern Stage/Edinburgh Lyceum/Nottingham Playhouse), *A Midsummer Night's Dream* (Wilton's Music Hall), *Lysistrata* (UK tour for Actors of Dionysus), *The Girl with the Iron Claws* (Arcola Theatre) and *Twelfth Night* (Rose Playhouse).

Film credits include: *Last Christmas* (Universal), *Last Train to Christmas* (Sky) and *Denial* (BBC Films).

TV credits include: *Sex Education* (Netflix), *Agatha Raisin* (Sky), *Starstruck* (HBO/BBC), *Good Omens* (Amazon/BBC), *Doctor Who* (BBC), *Black Mirror* (Netflix), *Lovesick* (Netflix) and *Silent Witness* (BBC).

James Westphal | Joe

James is a neurodiverse actor, writer and musician based in West London.

Theatre credits include: *Driftwood* (Pentabus and ThickSkin), *A-Typical Rainbow* (Turbine Theatre, Aria Entertainment), *Other Hands* (Bridewell Theatre, TuffLuv Theatre), *The Sam Wanamaker Festival* (The Globe), *A Wake In Progress* (Edinburgh Fringe, Fine Mess Theatre) and *Child of Science* (Bush Theatre, R&D).

Screen credits include: *Who_You, The Paramedics* (TV), *You Got A Face On* (Liftoff, Pinewood), *Sweetheart* (Met Film School), *Honey* (Short Film) and *In June* (Music Video).

James' play *Better Yet?* was also shortlisted for the *Original Theatre Playwriting Award* for 2022 and is currently in the process of being developed.

Royce Cronin | Ross

Royce is an actor and musician who trained at the Oxford School of Drama.

Theatre credits include: *The Little Prince* (Omnibus Theatre), *The Court Must Have A Queen* (Historic Royal Palaces), *Kicking and Screaming* (Tangled Feet), *Turf* (Kings Head Theatre), *The Hypochondriac* (Theatre Royal Bath), *Woyzeck* (Omnibus Theatre), *The Rubenstein Kiss* (Soho Theatre), *Imogen* (Arcola) and *The Fetch* (The Old Red Lion).

Film credits include: Royce can most recently be seen in the feature film *Gran Turismo* (Sony) and before that in *Bohemian Rhapsody* (20th Century Fox).

TV credits include: *Doctors* (BBC), *Holy Land Foundation* (Noon Films), *Boom!* (Snap B TV), *D-Day Landings* (BBC), *The Marchioness* (Granada), *24 Seven* (Granada Kids) and *Family Affairs* (FremantleMedia).

Creative Team

Barney Norris | Writer and Director

Barney Norris' work has received awards from the International Theatre Institute, the Critics' Circle, the *Evening Standard*, the Society of Authors as well as South Bank Sky Arts Times Breakthrough Awards, among others, and been translated into nine languages. His plays include *Visitors*, *Eventide*, *Nightfall*, *The Wellspring* and adaptations of Kazuo Ishiguro's *The Remains of the Day* and Federico García Lorca's *Blood Wedding*. His novels include *Undercurrent* and *Five Rivers Met on a Wooded Plain*. He will be the Green Party candidate for his hometown of Salisbury at the coming general election.

Becci Kenning | Designer

Becci Kenning is a visual artist and creative practitioner based in Surrey. Her practice is multidisciplinary and she specialises in large scale digital print collage. She established Art in Transit in 2009. Her work has been used in murals, fabric design, installations, exhibitions and theatre design.

Becci's previous theatre design work includes *Moonbrella* (2019) and *Emil and the Detectives* (2023). Becci trained at Wimbledon School of Art and Dartington College of Performing Arts. The majority of Becci's arts practice is community based with a strong co-authored content.

She is currently exhibiting at Croydon Clocktower Gallery as part of a Croydon Heritage project *Little Manhattan*, commissioned by Digital Drama.

Web: art-in-transit.com Instagram: @_artintransit

Tom Cook | Musical Director

Tom is a multi-instrumental composer, creator and performer who writes for TV (Netflix, BBC, ITV and Channel 4), online, live performance and gigs. He has worked for 30 years with different communities building shows, songs and cherishing the culture they create.

As part of Feral Theatre, Tom performed live/ableton at shows and a TED talk based around extinction.

He has been part of street performances, small theatre and co-writing *Debbie Rock Angel*, the first learning disabled rock opera, with Carousel Brighton.

As well as writing in his studio Tom works with Culture Shift running *Voices From the Edge*: sessions for writing and recording music with young people with and without neuro-diversity.

'This show has been so exciting as we took some time to write songs with the actors to create the feeling of a real band. I hope people resonate with that idea of going back to a time when life was less complicated even though the reality isn't as easy!'

Joshua Sanderson | Lighting Consultant

Josh has helped out with shows at Farnham Maltings for the past two years, making lights flash in shows including the latest Christmas show, *The Christmas Lobster*. He is currently studying Production Arts at Guildhall School of Music & Drama.

Vicki Cox | Stage Manager

Vicki trained at Falmouth University and has worked as technical stage manager on *Bal Maiden Musical* (Cobb, Riddle and Spall Music), *Come Out Fighting* (What Now Productions), *Bunker Cabaret* (Hooligan Arts Community), *Dido's Bar* (Dash Arts), *Treasure Island, Everyman, Sleeping Beauty* (Miracle Theatre), *Meet Me at the Edge* (Wildworks Theatre), *The Trench* (Collective Arts and Bodmin DCLI Museum), *Dracula, Duffy, It's Your Round, Game On and The Mayven Festival* (Scary Little Girls), *The Zig Zag Way* (Collective Arts & Trebiggan Production) and *A Curious Evening of Trance and Rap, A Great Dark Gathering* (Trifle Gathering Productions).

Vicki has also stage-managed stages at events run by Quick Panda Productions, Arc Live Ltd, ILOWHQ Ltd, Holifair Festival and has managed venues at private events and festivals throughout the UK (Glastonbury, Womad, Shambala, Boomtown). Vicki was also production manager for *The St Just Ordinalia* in 2021.

When not working with theatre companies she works in the Hall for Cornwall as a casual technician. Vicki can also be found on the stage in a cabaret act called *Wayne and Wanda* and also performs with her band The Disappointments.

farnham **maltings**

Farnham Maltings is a pioneering cultural organisation based in Surrey. Our ambition is to nurture the ecology of independent, contemporary theatre in the South East, connecting artists and audiences locally, nationally and globally.

We produce and tour theatre shows to village halls, community spaces, libraries and theatres around the UK and abroad. We are keen to explore new approaches to theatre, supporting artists and projects which encourage new forms and experiences which stealthily draw new audiences. These may be digital projects, work made to be staged in libraries, immersive experiences in cafes, or just a cracking story which delights its audiences.

Farnham Maltings' past productions include *The Christmas Lobster* (2023), *The Syrian Baker* (2019/2022), which won Play of the Year at the Writers' Guild of Great Britain Awards, *Brilliance*, and the critically acclaimed *Jess and Joe Forever* (2016), which transferred to the Orange Tree Theatre in Richmond after a successful UK tour.

Farnham Maltings supports theatre makers, producers and programmers to make their best work. We develop innovative and inspiring theatre that reflects our belief in the restorative power of the arts.

Farnham Maltings
Bridge Square
Farnham
Surrey
GU9 7QR

farnhammaltings.com

theatre@farnhammaltings.com

X 𝐟 ⃝ @farnhammaltings

Registration No. 954753 Charity No. 305034

Supported using public funding by

farnham **maltıngs**

Community Touring

Would you like us to visit your community?

If you've enjoyed tonight's show, and would like to see it performed in your venue, we'd love to hear from you. Farnham Maltings specialises in making theatre to be performed amongst communities; you'll find us in community centres and libraries, village halls and shopping malls. We're passionate about bringing good times to local communities and making shows that folk can pop down to and share with their neighbours. A great night out on your doorstep.

We work closely with venue managers to find the right show for them, and provide high quality marketing materials and expert advice on selling the show to the local community. Created alongside leading theatre-makers, our year-round programme of work offers a wide range of shows, catering to audiences of all ages and backgrounds. If you'd like to bring a performance of entertaining theatre to your community venue, follow the QR code below to find more information or get in touch via: **theatre@farnhammaltings.com**

'One of the best evening's entertainment I can remember' – audience member on *Brilliance*, Farnham Maltings (2018)

'Thank you so much for bringing us such an incredibly moving experience last night... it was extraordinary' – audience member on *The Syrian Baker*, Farnham Maltings (2022)

For Farnham Maltings

Chief Executive Officer
Peter Glanville
Executive Producer & Deputy CEO
Katy Potter
Interim Executive Director
Emma Haigh

Theatre
Producer
William Arnold
Community Touring Coordinator
Maria Rayner
Theatre Administrator
Eloise Talbot-Hammond
Community Producer (Social & Wellbeing)
Harriet Thompson
International Development Manager
Samantha Wood
house Touring Associate
Mark Makin
house Marketing Manager
Ellie Russell
house Administrator
Meghan Cosgrove

Craft
Craft Coordinators
Jo Connolly
Madeleine Harding
Caroline Pearce
Market Manager
Suzie Petcher

Programming
Programmer
Sophie Easterbrook
Producer (Programming & Artist Development)
Gina Thorley
Programming Administrator
Alice Morgan

Finance and HR
HR Manager
Rosie Bunnage
Finance Manager
Brice Hoskins
Executive Assistant
Paula Cairns

Finance Officer (Sales Ledger)
Rachel Bole
Finance Officer (Purchase Ledger)
Heidi Martin

Marketing
Development Director
Cordelia Wren
Communications & Marketing Manager
Jonathon Summers-Mileman
Communications & Marketing Officer
Sarah George
Marketing Officer
Olivia Hardy

Box Office
Senior Front of House Manager
Rose Woods
Sales Ticketing & Audience Manager
Jodi Bailey
Front of House Managers/Box Office Assistants
Olivia Aylott
Clare Ambrose
Alison Kirkpatrick
Victoria Pratt
Beth Tuppen
Casual Front of House Manager
Amanda Muir
Box Office Assistants
Jackie Kirk
Boris Allenou
Judith Needham
Eleanor Thomas
Suzie Petcher

Venue Operations
Head of Operations
Sara Lee
Venue Coordinator
Caroline Dinning
Duty Supervisor
Barry Taylor
Duty Officer
Chris Thompson
Jack Ashley
Nico Argenti
Tim Shurville

The Band Back Together

Barney Norris's work has received awards from the International Theatre Institute, the Critics' Circle, the Evening Standard, the Society of Authors and the South Bank Sky Arts Times Breakthrough Awards, among others, and been translated into nine languages. His plays include *Visitors*, *Eventide*, *Nightfall*, *The Wellspring* and adaptations of Ishiguro's *The Remains of the Day* and Lorca's *Blood Wedding*; his novels include *Undercurrent* and *Five Rivers Met on a Wooded Plain*. He will be the Green Party candidate for his home town of Salisbury at the coming general election.

BARNEY NORRIS

The Band Back Together

and

A Stranger Comes to Town

faber

First published in 2024
by Faber and Faber Limited
The Bindery, 51 Hatton Garden
London, EC1N 8HN

Typeset by Brighton Gray
Printed and bound in the UK by CPI Group (Ltd), Croydon CR0 4YY

A CIP record for this book
is available from the British Library

ISBN 978-0-571-39191-2

Printed and bound in the UK on FSC® certified paper in line with our continuing
commitment to ethical business practices, sustainability and the environment.
For further information see faber.co.uk/environmental-policy

2 4 6 8 10 9 7 5 3 1

The Band Back Together was first performed at Farnham Maltings on 8 March 2024, with the following cast:

Joe James Westphal
Ellie Laura Evelyn
Ross Royce Cronin

Director Barney Norris
Designer Becci Kenning
Musical Director Tom Cook
Lighting Consultant Joshua Sanderson
Company Stage Manager Vicki Cox

For Jeb, Matt and Rosie

Characters

Joe
thirties

Ellie
thirties

Ross
thirties

Setting

The play takes place in a village hall.

THE BAND BACK TOGETHER

Act One

1

A village hall. A keyboard, a drum kit, guitar stands, guitars. Somewhere in the space there's a second space with a kitchen – it doesn't matter where this is, or whether the performers have to pass through the audience to get to it. Joe enters with three coffees. He puts them down. He sits, clears his throat, plays a song, accompanying himself on the piano. Ellie enters while he plays. When he realises she's there, he stops.

Ellie Don't stop!

Joe Oh –

Ellie For me. Hello.

She opens her arms. They hug.

Joe You look exactly the same.

Ellie I'm literally twice the age I was when we were last in here.

Joe You look the same though.

Ellie Whereas you look dreadful.

Joe Thanks.

Ellie No, really, what happened? God I'm incredibly nervous. Nice to see you!

Joe And you, mate! I got you a coffee.

Joe goes to where he put the coffees down.

Ellie You're nice.

Joe That's what everyone says, but they're wrong.

Ellie Are they?

Joe It's a front. When I'm alone and no one can see me I'm very cruel to animals to balance it out.

Ellie Are you?

Joe I boil dogs, yeah. You can have a latte or a cappuccino. I got one of each. Ross gets the other.

Ellie Service station?

Joe No, I got 'em in town.

Ellie From the shop?

Joe It's gone downhill.

Ellie Of course it has.

Joe They actually literally haven't refurbished since we left. It's rotting around them.

Ellie You remember the milk down the back of the fridges?

Joe How do you even get milk down the back of a fridge?

Ellie We managed it all the time.

Joe But I never knew how. I quite fancy the manager now.

Ellie Is it not Ken?

Joe No.

Ellie Are you serious?

Joe Yeah.

Ellie Are you serious?

Joe I am.

Ellie Are you serious? I thought that man would always be the manager. Governments would come and go, and ice caps would melt, and he would simply continue. Managing. Or whatever it was he really did.

Joe He had that weed farm.

Ellie No, it was his friend's.

Joe That was it.

Ellie He was visiting his friend's weed farm when the police raided it, and he got out the window and his friend didn't, so he offered to run it till his friend got out in sort of solidarity.

Joe Why did the police not shut it down?

Ellie The weed farm?

Joe You'd think if the police had raided the place there wouldn't be a weed farm left to look after.

Ellie Maybe there was more than one.

Joe Must be it. A franchise. He runs the Jobcentre now.

Ellie Yeah?

Joe I went to see him.

Ellie Why?

Joe I dunno. I couldn't believe it. I thought he'd never leave there either.

Ellie Yeah.

Joe So I went in to see him, but I walked in the door and people were so hostile to me.

Ellie How do you mean?

Joe They marched me back out.

Ellie Of the Jobcentre?

Joe You have to have appointments. I think they thought I was gonna strip off or something.

Ellie Do an *I, Daniel Blake*.

Joe Does he do that?

Ellie Something like that. I haven't seen it.

Joe Wees all over everything.

Ellie Something like that. So you didn't see him?

Joe They said he was in a meeting.

Ellie And he doesn't run the café any more?

Joe No, it's someone else.

Ellie And you fancy her.

Joe She's friendly. I have this terrible affliction around people who are nice to me. Very common in men. It affects approximately one in two men. I just fall in love with anyone who's nice to me. Can't even help it. Someone smiles at me, I don't sleep for weeks.

Ellie I've seen that in you.

Joe There you go.

Ellie In my experience it's actually probably more than one in two men, so don't feel bad.

Joe Okay. It's sort of like baldness then. Comes to nearly all of us.

Ellie Yeah, I guess it is. I'll have the cap.

Joe Cool.

He gives her a coffee. She sips it.

Ellie That is stone cold and not in a good way.

Joe I got here early. You don't have to drink it.

Ellie No, it's all right. If you tell yourself it's meant to taste like that it's almost bearable.

Joe Like life.

Ellie Exactly. Thank you, Joe, I appreciate it. I go back in sometimes too.

Joe Yeah?

Ellie When I'm back to see Mum. It's funny. They don't know who I am. I feel like a spy, like I'm there incognito. And I keep getting older and they stay the same age.

Joe Right?!

Ellie It's all kids in the exact same life stage we were at when we were there. It's quite charged, really. Imagine. The same pheromones all the time in that room, just different bodies passing through and pumping them out one after the other. It's beautiful. There must always be someone falling in love there. And someone preparing to come out to their parents. And someone saving to go round the world. And whatever other shit we did when we were young.

Joe Blackout drinking.

Ellie Yeah, that's what we did. Then make beds out of bags of coffee beans in the basement and pass out down there.

Joe I never went round the world.

Ellie It's overrated.

Joe I bet it's not.

Ellie I was being nice. I don't think you'd like it, to be fair.

Joe The world?

Ellie All the travel. You were never good at that. What?! You didn't like buses. You wouldn't have crisps in your bag because they rustled.

Joe That did really annoy me, crisps in my bag.

Ellie I know.

Joe That doesn't mean I wouldn't have liked the world.

Ellie Just the little trays and waiting at airports. Lots of it is actually waiting at airports.

Joe Maybe it's a good thing I stayed home then. And why go round India when there's so much of Wiltshire I still haven't seen?

Ellie Exactly.

Joe We've got as many ancient monuments as anywhere else.

Ellie And that's just the people who drink in the pubs!

Joe Funny!

Ellie I *am* funny, thank you! Thank you for noticing.

They both drink their coffees.

Joe Nice cold coffee.

Ellie Nice awkward silence.

Joe Sorry.

Ellie What for? Two to tango. How have you been?

Joe Well. Yeah. I guess –

Ellie Big question.

Joe Well, it's been a while.

Ellie Sorry.

Joe What for? What about you, how have you been?

Beat.

Ellie You kind of have to say everything or like, two words, don't you.

Joe That's it.

Ellie So.

Joe Yeah.

Ellie Everything seems like quite a lot now I'm weighing it up.

Joe Maybe build up to it.

Ellie Yeah, I'll take a run up. Not that there's like. A big story or anything. I mean I'm fine, I've been fine, there's no story. I just think the longer version takes a long time to tell. Like, we had the Olympics didn't we, remember that? I went to some of it. In the big stadium. And then there was all the really unexpected grief I felt when David Bowie died, I'd have to tell you about that. And how I got better at budgeting. There's been loads of stuff happened, you know? Could take ages to explain it all.

Joe But you're all right?

Ellie I'm all right.

Joe Well that's good then.

Ellie What a relief eh?

Joe All the same limbs I remember so well.

Ellie Several of the same teeth. I've survived this long.

Joe And that ain't nothin'.

Ellie Mozart didn't.

Joe Kurt Cobain. I'm the same age as Lorca was when they shot him.

Ellie In India in 1900, life expectancy was thirty-three, and we're past that. And half of the world's population are under twenty-five today. So that might actually make us top forty per cent. Or bottom forty per cent. But old, anyway.

Joe We're nailing it by every empirical measure.

Ellie God yes! And you're living back here?

Joe Yeah.

Ellie Me too.

Joe Really?

Ellie Nearly. I'm just coming back.

Joe Oh, wow. I didn't know.

Ellie Me and my partner are thinking it's time to try and pop out a sprog, you know? So we're gonna rinse Mum for free babysitting.

Joe Nice.

Ellie And the schools and the life and London's a hellhole and all the other more sincere stuff one might say if one were more emotionally intelligent and not feeling a bit shy and overwhelmed, obviously.

Joe Obviously. Are you?

Ellie What?

Joe Feeling. Overwhelmed.

Ellie Only a bit. It'll pass.

Joe Me too if it helps.

Ellie Yeah? That's good. Solidarity.

> *They clink cups.*

Joe Good to see you though.

Ellie Yeah. Good and horrible.

Joe Why?

Ellie Time and stuff, innit.

Joe Stephen Hawking's original working title.

Ellie I believe it was. It's good to see you too.

> *They're not exactly drowning in things to say.*

So I'm moving home, yeah.

Joe Are we pretending we're grown-ups in a room making conversation?

Ellie I think so, yeah!

Joe Have we become strangers?

Ellie Maybe just at first.

Joe Bloody hell.

Ellie If we keep going it might get better.

Joe Okay. So, are you buying somewhere?

Ellie Edge of town. Where are you?

Joe On Wilton Road.

Ellie We're gonna be on the other side, on Elm Grove?

Joe I don't know it.

Ellie It's just a little flat. We fit in it. So . . .

Joe Always a plus.

Ellie This is good pretending, isn't it?

Joe Yeah, we're nailing it. Do you wanna tell me about the property prices in the area, is that what people talk about now when they're grown-ups? Or the schools?

Ellie A big part of me wants to shout at the top of my voice, 'I've seen you naked but now it's been years since we saw each other and for some reason that is extremely upsetting,' but maybe we'll get to that later, you know?

Joe Okay.

Ellie They found hand axes in the basement. In the building where I'm buying my flat.

Joe Yeah?

Ellie They're in the Museum in the Close, you can go and look at them. If you want. You don't have to. They're meant to be three hundred thousand years old. I might have got the decimal point in the wrong place, but that's the number in my head.

Joe Ancient monuments.

Ellie Right?

Joe Good callback. That is amazing, to be fair.

Ellie I think so actually.

Joe Were people using axes back then?

Ellie They were on Elm Grove, mate. Fighting off the sabre-tooth tigers of Laverstock.

Joe Hunting the wolves of Milford Hollow. It's not wrong.

Ellie What?

Joe The decimal point. It's about ice ages. Half a million years back there were people in England. Then a few more a quarter of a million years later. And then again for the last ten thousand years. But none in between because the place was frozen.

Ellie Oh right.

Joe We turn up now and then.

Ellie Fair enough.

Joe The oldest thing anyone ever found in England was footprints dating back a million years ago. On a beach in Norfolk. Or somewhere like that. Essex, maybe, this bit of land fell in the sea and exposed these footsteps. They could tell the age from the depth or something. But they only lasted a few weeks once they were in the open. The rain got to them. Sorry, boring.

Ellie No.

Joe Little bit.

Ellie What were you playing when I came in?

Joe Oh, just a song.

Ellie Really? I thought it was a game of mah-jong.

Joe Yeah, but I'm shy.

Ellie Not really.

Joe Why not?

Ellie I was five minutes late, yeah? You started playing music more or less when we were due to arrive. Now Ross still isn't here, Ross is properly late. But we're all grown-ups now, we all have jobs. So we're basically likely to turn up on time because all that being chaotic, it got old, didn't it. We can't get away with it any more. We're frankly not pretty enough to be excused it now we're into the dregs of our thirties. I just got caught up at that roadworks for a minute.

Joe Oh, yeah.

Ellie Pointless. Why are there so many potholes now?

Joe Like to a tenement or pelting slum.

Ellie What?

Joe Don't worry.

Ellie But here's the thing. Every bar you played of your song made it more likely I'd come in and hear you while you were singing. Me or Ross. Cos one of us was always gonna be basically on time. So you're not shy. You wanted someone to hear you. So tell me about your song.

Joe It's just a song. I just got anxious. Like you have a party and you think no one'll come.

Ellie Were you that child?

Joe No.

Ellie I bet you were that child.

Joe You weren't.

Ellie I threw legendary parties. Still do.

Joe Thanks for the invites.

Ellie You'll get some now I'm coming home. I'm gonna stop drinking this now, it's so horrible.

Joe Sorry.

Ellie No, I appreciate the gesture. I'll chuck it down the sink. You done with yours?

Joe Sure.

Ellie One sec.

Ellie exits with both cups. Joe goes to the piano, looks at it, looks up at where Ellie left, then doesn't play it. He gets out his phone and starts texting. Ellie comes back in.

You texting him?

Joe Just in case there's a problem.

Ellie He'll be coming down from town will he?

Joe I guess so.

Ellie Is he staying with his parents?

Joe He didn't say really. I think so.

Ellie They had a nice bloody house. Have you been sick in his downstairs loo?

Joe Yeah.

Ellie I reckon half of Salisbury's been sick in his downstairs loo, they let him have so many parties. Happy days.

Joe Yeah.

Ellie They will never come again.

Joe Oh.

Ellie We'll have a different sort of happy now with less throwing up.

Joe Oh, yeah.

Ellie Living with anyone?

Joe No, just me.

Ellie Seeing anyone?

Joe Not at the moment.

Ellie Boring!

Joe Sorry.

Ellie You have to feed me gossip!

Joe I haven't got a lot.

Ellie Working in town?

Joe Don't laugh, right?

Ellie Go on.

Joe I actually work at Games Workshop.

Ellie Are you joking?

Joe I tried to deny it for years, but I love it, El. I really love making little model men. And I know that's sad, and implies some kind of tragic extended adolescence, and a failure to engage with the actual world. But I reached an age when life felt too short for me to pretend I don't love little model men any more. And they advertised for an assistant manager and I thought, I actually think that's me. I think that's who I actually am. So now I paint little model men all day, and train other people to paint little model men, and then at night I go home and play with my train set, which is not a joke, it's not even a euphemism, I have a magnificent train set, and I am so bloody madly happy I don't even care that I'm

25

basically undateable. Because I've got my little model trains and my little model men. When I was growing up me and my brother had loads of it. Little orcs and all that. And then one day when I'd joined the band, I thought to myself, you have to cut this out. If you ever want to have friends and be normal, there cannot be wizards. You must cut out this part of your life and then bury it. And me and my brother, we threw it all away. Hundreds of quid of orcs and goblins. Hundreds of hours with the radio playing while we painted them all different shades of green. All in the bin like it never happened. But that was the real me. And I'm taking him back.

Ellie You've dug up the body.

Joe I've sewn the arm back on.

Ellie Well now I have a dilemma, don't I.

Joe Yeah?

Ellie Cos that screams cry for help. I'm just being honest. That is absolutely tragic. But we're all meant to encourage our friends to be their true selves, aren't we. Battle re-enactments? You go girl! Drinking while pregnant? Live your best life! So maybe while you're clearly in need of an intervention, conventional wisdom currently requires that instead of literally sectioning you right now, I politely ask if you have any photos of your favourite little model men?

Joe I do actually.

Ellie Of course you do.

Joe I'm in some pretty competitive WhatsApp groups.

Ellie Do you send each other photos of your little model men?

Joe Living my best life like you said.

Ellie Do you find quite a lot of your friendship group are also male and single?

Joe It's weird that, isn't it?

Ellie It really is.

Joe Do you actually want to see any of my –

Ellie I'd rather you sent me a dick pic, Joe.

Joe I don't think people do that any more.

Ellie No?

Joe I think that was just men getting excited when the camera phone first got invented.

Ellie That's how men show their excitement the world over, isn't it. Knob out, bit of helicoptering. Half of Wembley stadium does it whenever England score, I'm led to believe. The main stand at Cheltenham's a sight on Gold Cup day.

Joe It's how we show joy.

Ellie That's why I've always got my tits out.

Joe You see? You understand!

Ellie We've got a lot of love to give.

Joe Speaking of which.

Ellie Yeah?

Joe You're gonna have a baby?

Ellie Well, that's the plan, yeah. That's the idea. Sort of just starting to hit 'now or never' time, aren't we. Well I am. You've clearly already chosen never with your little model men.

Joe It's mad, isn't it.

Ellie If we'd had a kid they'd be eighteen now.

Joe Bloody hell. Isn't that amazing?

Ellie It's a different life. I'm not sure it would be a worse one.

Joe If you and I had had a kid?

Ellie Maybe not us specifically. But I don't feel old now. I've got life left in me. Imagine if the parenting was basically done, and I was just about to get back to free living! Maybe that would have been the better way round. Except I'd have had to have a baby with you.

Joe We'd have been all right.

Ellie Yeah, we would probably.

Joe Or we'd have separated and I'd have been a weekend dad.

Ellie Taking some resentful little snot to the zoo who went home and wrote poems about how he hated you. Do you want kids?

Joe Oh.

Ellie Sorry, is that –

Joe No, you just caught me off balance.

Ellie So?

Joe Do I want kids?

Ellie Yeah.

Joe I don't know. It feels like an abstract question.

Ellie Because you're single?

Joe Maybe, yeah. God, it's weird isn't it. Five years ago I never had this conversation. Now we've been stood here ten minutes and we're already into it.

Ellie Sorry!

Joe No, it's interesting. It's a 'life stage' thing.

Ellie Costa was all about sexual positions. These days we're all about fertility cycles.

Joe You can have both.

Ellie You *can* have both.

Joe checks his phone.

Joe Ross hasn't texted back.

Ellie Too soon to talk about sexual positions?

Joe Apparently. I don't know when I got this shy.

Ellie You were always this shy. I liked that about you. I like that about you, present tense.

Joe Thanks. I like your lifelong ability to make me feel uncomfortable.

Ellie Why?

Joe There are different layers of us, aren't there? So at the same time as I'm feeling shy and checking my phone now, there's another me sort of watching that from above, and laughing, because that's exactly how we worked. Always, all along, that was us. You were much less scared of things than me. And we used to be in love, and now we haven't seen each other in ten years, and it's weirdly upsetting to meet again, but I don't mind actually because I do like you.

Ellie Gimme a hug.

They hug.

I missed you. Play me something.

Joe El.

Ellie That's why we're here, isn't it?

Joe When he gets here.

Ellie He might not come.

Joe He'd tell me if he'd cancelled.

Ellie Do you think he would?

Joe You play me something.

Ellie I can't play the piano. I was Stevie Nicks, remember? Me and my tambourine. Girls weren't really allowed in the bands. That was problematic. Like having to play hockey instead of football. And Home Ec. And you not having Home Ec. Our childhoods were entirely problematic.

Joe You can play *something*, surely?

Ellie Probably not, mate. I haven't picked up one of those in years. Go on. Play what you were playing.

Joe I haven't warmed up.

Ellie Then this is your warm-up.

Joe All right.

Joe plays a song.

There you go.

Ellie Hated it.

Joe Thanks.

Ellie I could tell you hadn't warmed up. No, it's nice.

Joe Thanks.

Ellie You still sound like you.

Joe I am me. More or less.

Ellie Are you?

Joe I think so.

Ellie I don't know whether I am. It's sort of lovely to be here and listening to you again.

Joe Yeah. It's emotional.

Ellie Yeah, it sort of is. Have you really booked an actual gig then?

Joe We can always bail if we can't play in time.

Ellie Will anyone come?

Joe I dunno. I hope so.

Ellie Where is it?

Joe Here.

Ellie Here?

Joe Like we used to.

Ellie No one will come, Joe.

Joe I think the local community's supportive.

Ellie Yeah, of like, good stuff. Bric-a-brac sales and choral singing and local elections and swingers' parties, not you and me messing about with a drum kit.

Joe You and me and Ross. And Ross is famous.

Ellie He's not famous.

Joe Because of that advert.

Ellie Do you think that advert's famous?

Joe Ross is like the Scottish Widow. He's the most famous person in my phone.

Ellie No he's not.

Beat.

He might be actually.

Joe Isn't he?

Ellie He might be. God that's depressing.

Joe Why?

Ellie When I was a kid here I felt so disconnected from the big wide world and everything in it. And I went to London and I was so certain that I was going to get out of this oxbow lake, and join society, and be a real person. But Ross might still be the most famous person in my phone.

Joe You never leave Salisbury.

Ellie Apparently not.

Joe Feet to the rising and setting may run, they always beat on the same small stone.

Ellie What?

Joe Don't worry.

Ellie So members of the public will come here to hear us perform music we make with our mouths and hands?

Joe In theory. It's for charity.

Ellie Is it? What charity?

Joe It's a novichok benefit.

Ellie Is it?

Joe That's why I first suggested it, remember?

Ellie Yeah, but, Joe, that was years ago now.

Joe Yeah. We delayed it cos of Covid. And cos Ross wouldn't play live cos he was anti-vax.

Ellie Is that why we didn't do it last year?

Joe Yeah.

Ellie Is he still anti-vax?

Joe I think he got over it. He went on the marches though.

Ellie Really?

Joe He said it was just to see what they were like. But I think he took a placard just to see what that was like, too.

Ellie What did it say?

Joe 'My body, my choice.'

Beat.

Ellie Well that could be worse.

Joe It could, to be fair.

Ellie Everyone went mental didn't they.

Joe *He* did.

Ellie If he talks about big pharma or conspiracies I'm leaving.

Joe (*unconvinced*) He won't talk about big pharma or conspiracies.

Beat.

Would you actually leave?

Ellie Just – not anti-Semitism. He can do a *bit* on big pharma if he absolutely has to. But no anti-Semitism. That's my line.

Joe I mean, it's a good line.

Ellie I think so, thank you. So this is a novichok benefit gig?

Joe Yeah.

Ellie Will anyone remember it?

Joe Novichok? Of course. The war in Ukraine started here in Salisbury.

Ellie Well, it didn't.

Joe You know what I mean though.

Ellie What charity are we fundraising for?

Joe I don't know yet. I looked up novichok charities in the area and it turns out there isn't one really.

Ellie Cos everyone forgot about it.

Joe No. I reckon there probably would have been one. People just got distracted by everything else.

Ellie Twenty-twenty.

Joe It's so disappointing because that was the best-named year.

Ellie It was.

Joe I was looking forward to it so much. The football season was gonna be called the twenty-twenty twenty-twenty-one season. How good is that? Twenty-twenty twenty-twenty-one. But I didn't enjoy it. Yet another thing that Covid took from me.

Ellie 'Two examiners were locked in a debate over whether a particular sentence required "had" or "had had" in order to correctly convey its meaning. The chief examiner, while her colleague had had "had", had had "had had"; "had had" had had the exam board's approval.'

Joe What's that?

Ellie If you like repeating words.

Joe That was meant to be a joke?

Ellie It's a sentence with the same word in it eleven times in a row!

Joe Should I laugh or clap, or – ?

Ellie I thought you'd like it!

Joe It is quite cool actually.

Ellie It's better than twenty-twenty twenty-twenty-one.

Joe It's not.

Ellie Eleven beats four.

Joe But yours isn't real. Roy Keane was gonna have to say mine again and again for a whole year. That's better than something you made up.

Ellie I don't know who Roy Keane is, Joe.

Joe Seriously?

Ellie Football's worse than Warhammer.

Joe Is it?

Ellie Oh, yeah. Football is the ick. We can pick a charity later I guess.

Joe Yeah. We'll just donate the door money to wherever.

Ellie Non-existent door money.

Joe People will come. People like charity stuff. People are mugs.

Ellie That's nice.

Joe I'm big hearted.

Ellie You're not just gonna play all your own depressing songs are you?

Joe Was that depressing?

Ellie Well.

Joe It's moving as well though.

Ellie Yeah, sure.

Joe Is it miserable?

Ellie It is a bit miserable. We should play things people can sing along to.

Joe I don't know anything people can sing along to.

Ellie Well this'll be fun then.

Joe It's the band back together.

Ellie Yes?

Joe So we have to play the old band music.

Ellie That wasn't one of ours.

Joe No, I wrote that since.

Ellie You'll bend the rules for that then.

Joe I didn't say that was in the gig.

Ellie What is then?

Joe What's in the gig?

Ellie Play me something. Play me a characteristic song from the night.

Joe Well I don't know what's going to be characteristic, we haven't got a set list. That's why we're rehearsing. We'll work out what we can all play.

Ellie Just set the mood for me. What kind of show will this be?

Joe I do know some covers.

Ellie Good. People like things they've heard of.

Joe I could play you a cover.

Ellie Go on.

Enter Ross, carrying a guitar and an amp.

Ross What are those temporary traffic lights about?!

Ellie Is that your excuse?

Ross Also I was late.

Ellie Unlike you.

Ross People don't change. Looks like you haven't.

Ellie Hello.

Ross Hello. All right, Joe, sorry.

Joe No, you're fine, mate. How are you doing?

Ross Yeah, I mean – fine, I guess.

Joe I got you a coffee.

Ross Oh. Thanks.

Ellie It was already cold ten minutes ago when I got here so good luck.

Ross Okay. Well that's my bad. There isn't a microwave?

Joe 'Fraid not, no.

Ellie Milk'd burn in a microwave.

Ross Would it?

Joe It could. If you left it too long.

Ross Well everything burns if you leave it too long.

Joe True. This is sort of not how I imagined this moment.

Ross No, fair point.

Ellie I imagine we all imagined our reunion with less milk.

Ross sips his cold coffee.

Ross This is horrible.

Joe Sorry.

Ross I might –

Ellie Kitchen's through there.

Ross I remember!

Ellie Sorry.

Ross Did you drink yours?

Ellie No.

Joe And hers wasn't as cold.

Ross Yeah, I might just –

Joe Go for it.

Ross exits to the kitchen.

Ross (*off*) They haven't refurbished since I was last in here!

Ellie Funny, isn't it!

Ross (*off*) Place is rotting around us.

Ellie This is so strange.

Joe You okay?

Ellie I thought it would feel more fun. It doesn't feel very fun at all.

Joe Yeah.

Ellie I just feel awkward. What are we gonna say?

Joe It'll be all right.

Ellie We could leave before he comes back in.

Joe We can't.

Ellie But we could.

Joe But we won't.

Ellie Will we not?

Joe Please stay.

Ellie The door's there.

Joe But it'll get better.

Ellie I'll stay for you.

Joe Thank you.

Ellie We're a team now aren't we.

Joe Yeah.

Ellie We're gonna help each other get through this.

Ross enters.

Ross You guys okay?

Ellie All good.

Ross Good to see you. Here we all are!

Ellie (*weakly*) Yeah!

Ross Don't we look older.

Ellie Thanks.

Ross Well, I'm twice the age I was when I was last here, I dunno 'bout you.

Ellie Obviously the same, Ross, because we're the same age.

Ross There you go then. That'd explain it. I had such a nightmare getting here. I was actually in Portugal till last night?

Joe I went to Portugal with you once.

Ross The Azores, yeah.

Joe For that gig.

Ross And we slept on the guitarist's floor.

Joe And his abs.

Ross I remember.

Joe He'll have been younger than we are now.

Ross Christ. That's so weird. You're right. I still know him.

Joe Yeah?

Ross We text.

Joe Is that why you were in –

Ross No, I had a gig. Just in someone else's band. You know, the backing band thing. That's the only way to make money now.

Ellie Well.

Ross Out of music I mean. I don't mean the entire world economy. You get in the band of someone famous, and they'll give you a fee, and that funds the fun stuff.

Ellie Cos streaming doesn't pay.

Ross Yeah.

Joe Ads do though.

Ross When you get them. If you get them.

Joe You had that one.

Ross Yeah, nine years ago. Doesn't get you through a whole entire life. You know the way Tom Waits got ahead was he sued some ad for cereal or something that ripped off his voice. They did a sort of impersonation, and he got two and a half million dollars. That's what you need. Not an ad, you need a lawsuit. What have you guys been doing?

Joe Well I was married.

Ellie What?

Joe Yeah.

Ross I sort of just meant today while I was late.

Joe Oh.

Ellie You were married?

Joe Yeah.

Ellie You didn't say.

Joe No. Sorry. I misunderstood. We started playing a little bit, didn't we.

Ellie No, hang on. When were you married?

Joe For about three years. Up until Covid.

Ellie Then you stopped being married.

Joe Yeah.

Ellie Bloody hell.

Joe Sorry, I wasn't trying to –

Ross What happened?

Joe We got divorced, yeah.

Ross Your idea or hers?

Joe Hers.

Ross Shit, man. I'm sorry.

Joe No, no. Sorry, I misunderstood your question.

Ellie I can't believe you didn't mention this!

Joe Yeah. It's kind of strange to talk about it. We got married and then she got ill? And when she got better she said we should call it. So yeah. That was my big thing. I was married. Had a little go at having a life. It didn't work out. Overrated!

Ellie And this is why the little model men.

Joe Yeah.

Ross What?

Ellie Don't worry.

Ross Are you still in touch?

Joe No.

Ross Fuck.

Joe We tried. It didn't work out. We weren't kind to each other.

Ellie That must be –

Joe Yeah.

Ross I'm sorry about that, man.

Joe You're not married to your partner, are you?

Ellie No, we haven't done it. We might. We haven't yet.

Ross Costs a lot.

Joe Yeah.

Ross Sorry.

Joe No, you're all right.

Ross And your ex was –

Joe She forgot who she was. There was more to it than that, but.

Ellie You don't have to talk about it.

Joe Thanks.

Ross Sorry, mate.

   Beat.

Well we've gone in off the high board, haven't we!

Joe Sorry.

Ross Eighteen years. It's weird what happens to you.

Joe Yeah.

Ross But you're with someone?

Ellie Yeah.

Joe They're moving back.

Ross To Salisbury?

Joe Three-hundred-thousand-year-old axe heads in the basement.

Ross That's cool.

Ellie Thanks, yeah.

Ross Is that what you talked about while you were waiting for me? Archaeology?

Ellie Well that's basically what this is, isn't it.

Ross Fair point. Why are you coming back?

Ellie Well. It's where my family are.

Joe And me.

Ellie And Joe, obviously. That was the main thing. I just wanted to be closer to Joe.

Ross I mean who doesn't?

Joe Apart from my ex-wife.

Ross I couldn't do it.

Joe Be close to me?

Ross Move back this way.

Ellie Why not?

Ross It's not my world now. This is the first time I've been in five years.

Ellie Your family are still here though.

Ross Yeah. I don't see them.

Ellie Oh.

Ross Usual family stuff. I'm staying there tonight. First time we've stayed under the same roof in. I dunno. In a very long time.

Ellie That's good.

Ross Is it? We'll have to see, won't we.

Joe I've got a sofa if it goes badly.

Ross Thanks, mate. Where are you?

Joe On the Wilton Road. Near the fire station.

Ross I like it round there. They have the fair.

Joe Yeah. I mean it tours around, but that's one of the places it stops, yeah.

Ross You haven't been here all the time since school though?

Joe Yeah.

Ross Fucking hell. Do we know your ex then?

Joe No. She was from Winchester.

Ross That explains it.

Joe Can't trust any of 'em.

Ross I am sorry though, mate.

Ellie Yeah.

Joe Thanks.

Beat.

Ellie Joe says that you're anti-vax.

Joe Bloody hell, El.

Ellie Well, it's funnier than this chat.

Ross I was a bit, actually. I got over it.

Ellie How come?

Ross I had a friend who died. You know, she got a blood clot after the booster. Which might not have been the booster. I don't know. But for a while after that I was pretty anti-vax.

Ellie This isn't much funnier than the last chat, actually.

Ross This is how it goes though. Once you're not young any more, when you meet up you end up talking about death. This is the least dead everyone in our lives will ever be from here on in.

Ellie Well that's a nice thought.

Ross I went on some marches. But they were all mental. I met people who actually wore tin foil hats. Literal actual people with literal tin foil on their head. I never thought it was real till then. I thought it was a joke or something. And everyone on the marches was completely obsessed with civilisation being much older than we realised. All they'd talk about was how the Sphinx's head in Egypt was too big for its body and that proved there'd been a giant flood. I mean, obviously there was a giant flood, the whole of geology is about the fact that there was a giant flood once, isn't it? But the people on the marches thought it proved we'd all been rocking out with tools way before it all happened for some reason. Not like, living in caves eating sticks or whatever. They were obsessed. The number of people who'd stare at me unblinking, these mad intense eyes, and tell me the Egyptians had electricity and they could prove it because they'd drawn a picture of it, or they had it tattooed on their arm and that was evidence, and it was kept from us because archaeology's all a conspiracy. I quite liked that. Like, Time Team are the real secret masters of the world. Tony Robinson working to keep us in the dark. I got sort of into it. Then I got out of it.

Ellie Because we were all locked up on our own, we became certain that we were missing out.

Ross And we were. But we thought about all the wrong things. We thought about conspiracies and Ancient Egyptians. It was ordinary life we missed. It was sitting having coffee with friends.

Joe Or not having coffee.

Ross If the coffee's really bad.

Ellie We're missing out now.

Ross How d'you mean?

Ellie Everything we do is lots of other things we don't. Anyway, depressing. What's the plan? Is it Sunday night, Joe, is that what we're doing?

Joe That's it. Rehearse today and tomorrow, then gig on Sunday.

Ross What time?

Joe Five.

Ross What do you mean, five?

Joe The gig's at five.

Ross Why?

Joe Well, it's Sunday evening.

Ross Yes?

Joe So Sunday dinner.

Ross What?

Joe We'll have an older audience.

Ross It's a gig, you can't start at five!

Ellie Just imagine you're low down the bill at Glasto.

Ross I don't want to be low down the bill at Glasto.

Ellie Better than you can manage in real life.

Joe All right, play nicely.

Ross Fair play though.

Ellie Thank you. Come on, shall we start?

Ross Yeah, why not?

Ross gets his guitar out.

Let me tune up.

Ross tunes up. Joe helps with notes on the piano.

It's like falling back into the past, doing this with you two.

Ellie Yeah.

Ross I remember the first time we played battle of the bands. And you wouldn't vote so we lost by one.

Joe Sorry.

Ross I remember getting in the back of your car and all of us going to Glasto, or London, or Manchester for a weekend away and a gig. I remember sleeping in Cheltenham parks so we could hear Herbie Hancock play. I remember dropping acid by the sea in the night, and you were there, and we started to sing. All of it's here.

Joe All the good and the bad.

Ross How we all fell apart.

Ellie How the three of us stopped talking. How suddenly one day there wasn't a band, and I missed that. I hadn't seen that coming.

Joe How I gave up and stayed behind. And seeing you both getting onto that train.

Ross How you and I didn't last past the first term of uni, and what we'd lost seemed bigger then than whatever we'd had.

Ellie But there was no way of getting it back.

Joe No way of putting the band back together.

Ross Not that we were all that good, anyway.

Joe Just like every other group of kids growing up in a small town.

Ross Just like any other kids who played guitar.

Ellie We were the same as everyone young in England. With a dream too big to ever quite happen.

Joe But a beautiful dream.

Ross For as long as it lasted.

Ellie A beautiful dream that shaped everything after.

Ross Because we all live in memory of the kids we were.

Ellie And try and do right by the kids we were. And try and do things with our lives they'd have approved of.

Ross Like coming back here.

Ellie Like coming back together.

Joe Like sitting in this place to make music again, even though it was only a dream, only silly.

Ross But not at the time. At the time it was everything.

Joe It just changed while we were growing up.

Ross When we were kids there were bands who made money.

Ellie Not any more by the time we left school.

Ross So we went our own ways and did something different.

Joe Not you.

Ross Me too. I sold out.

Ellie You didn't.

Ross I wrote music for ads and played on pop songs. That wasn't who I was going to be.

Joe We were proud of you though. We would have liked to tell you.

Ellie But it was hard to keep in touch.

Ross After the break-ups.

Ellie And the band ended.

Ross And people would text and I'd mean to text back.

Ellie And it was too hard to know what to say really. There was too much. So I just said nothing.

Ross Because we were young once. There used to be just future.

Joe But time keeps happening, though you try to slow it.

Ellie You get one youth and ours is over.

Lights change. The three play a song together.
Interval.

Act Two

Ross is set up with his guitar. Ellie enters.

Ellie Hey.

Ross Oh, hi.

Ellie How was your night?

Ross All right.

Ellie No drama?

Ross Just sort of awkward. Nothing went wrong. It's just sad. Cos the moment's passed, hasn't it. We can patch things up and whatever. But we're never gonna be actually close again. That broke. That's gone. I'm an adult. The moment for happy families passed.

Ellie I know what you mean.

Ross But you don't agree?

Ellie I think it's only passed if you decide it has.

Ross By the time they're eighteen, ninety per cent of the time the average person will spend with their family has already happened.

Ellie Really?

Ross Apparently we've got like, two or three per cent left.

Ellie I mean that's so depressing.

Ross Unless you haven't enjoyed the ninety-seven or ninety-eight per cent you've already had.

Ellie Joe not here yet? Strange.

Ross I thought so. Think this is more him than us, don't you?

Ellie Well, it was his idea.

Ross Exactly. What?

Ellie What?

Ross Why are you pissed at me?

Ellie I'm not.

Ross Yeah but you are though.

Ellie I'm not pissed at you, Ross. We're not fifteen.

Ross You are though. Go on. Say what you're thinking.

Ellie I just think when they're elderly they might still need you. That might be another time for happy families.

Ross Sorry?

Ellie Your parents. And I don't think it works like that.

Ross Like what?

Ellie There are no happy families. You either choose to keep going or you sort of give up. It doesn't equal happiness. It's just love.

Ross Yeah, I suppose so.

Ellie Sorry.

Ross No, fine. Anyway. Yesterday was good.

Ellie Yeah, it was.

Ross I wasn't sure what to expect. But we sounded all right. And it's fun, getting all that out again.

Ellie Some things.

Ross What?

Ellie Some of it's more fun than others.

Ross I just meant the songs.

Ellie Oh, sorry.

Ross No, fine. I know what you mean about the other –

Ellie Yeah, right.

Ross But we're cool, are we?

Ellie Yeah. I think so.

Ross Well I think we're cool too.

Ellie Well then, that's all right. It brought back a lot of happy memories, singing with you.

Ross Yeah?

Ellie You and Joe. I loved it.

Ross Yeah, I loved it.

Ellie I mean I loved being in that band. Not even gigging necessarily, just the group, the feeling of the group, the togetherness. That was there again for me yesterday. I didn't really imagine it would be. I think for a lot of people, when they love a particular band, when they're really into a particular band, that's a big part of what they fall in love with. Yes, the music, but the bond as well. The idea of those kids all together, and never growing up somehow, never growing out of that feeling that life's about having adventures with your friends. Because everyone has those friendships. You don't have to be musical to have had those incredibly intense adolescent friendships.

Ross I think it's about sex too. Sex as well as friendship.

Ellie Well you would, wouldn't you.

Ross Why?

Ellie Ross.

Ross I didn't mean that.

Ellie No?

Ross I wasn't just being smutty.

Ellie Go on then.

Ross What?

Ellie Explain. Keep digging.

Ross Well I had a friend saw the Beatles live. And before they came on she was saying to herself, I'm not like this riff-raff, I'm here for the music, I'm not just here to scream at the top of my voice because I fancy them. Then they walked on stage and this wave hit her, and she said she screamed at the top of her voice for an hour like everyone else till they walked back off and she hadn't heard them play a note.

Ellie It's just love. It's very Fleetwood Mac, being in a band is a very intense way of being in love.

Ross Yeah.

Ellie Anyway. I hope Joe's okay.

Ross Do you?

Ellie What?

Ross If he didn't turn up we could do something else.

Ellie It's Saturday morning, Ross, don't try and seduce me.

Ross Sex doesn't have to happen at night.

Ellie Mate, I'm so not interested.

Ross Fair play, all right. It's fun though isn't it.

Ellie What?

Ross Being back in a room together.

Ellie I'm not feeling the same way you're feeling.

Ross All right. You remember when we'd practise in my garage?

Ellie Yes.

Ross I loved that. That deafening sound. Worst imaginable acoustics to rehearse in. And my dad parking his soft-top on the drive, and if it rained he'd reverse back in even while we were playing.

Ellie He loved that car.

Ross Yeah!

Ellie To the extent that he'd reverse over his only son to save it.

Ross That sounded almost biblical.

Ellie That's sort of what God did, yeah. If the car was the world and you were Jesus.

Ross I've sometimes imagined I might be.

Ellie No you haven't. You've imagined you were chocolate, I'll give you that. But if you relate to any biblical character, you and I both know that it's Satan.

Ross That is who I relate to, you're right. Better to reign in hell and all that.

Ellie I remember.

Ross Bet you do.

Ellie Ross!

Ross I'm only mucking around.

Ellie Well don't.

Ross Is anyone gonna come to this gig then?

Ellie I dunno. I can't imagine they will. Anyone we knew has kids or lives in London, the kids round here now won't want to listen to us, and the actual locals never liked us anyway.

Ross There used to be a good scene. I dunno whether it's the same now. You could get gigs all over. Southampton and Bournemouth and Poole, I don't think we ever played Portsmouth did we?

Ellie Frome, and Bristol, never as far as Cardiff.

Ross And closer to home. Warminster and Trowbridge. I liked all that. I liked going to different places. Always thought that was one of the compensations of the life. I mean it's so fucking hard most of the time, but you get that, you do get to travel.

Ellie Do Warminster and Trowbridge count as travel?

Ross You know what I mean, I mean good nights out. It was sort of about how much money we had for petrol really, because if you could afford the fuel, you could get on the bottom of a bill and play somewhere.

Ellie And you could play Salisbury. Along with all the ska punk.

Ross I hated ska punk.

Ellie I don't know why there was so much of it.

Ross Brighton once, we played a gig in Brighton.

Ellie Was that the first time you ever went?

Ross Yeah, it was actually.

Ellie Well then.

Ross What?

Ellie You have us to thank for that.

Ross Why?

Ellie Well you live there now don't you?

Ross Yeah.

Ellie That's cos of us then.

Ross I mean maybe.

Ellie I was joking.

Ross I do remember it, to be fair. I was sort of excited about it. It felt like a big deal because Brighton was like, a proper place. No offence to everywhere else, but it is, it's a proper place.

Ellie I get you.

Ross Too dear now. I'm getting priced out.

Ellie Are you?

Ross My flatmates are thinking of moving.

Ellie Where to?

Ross Hastings.

Ellie Long bloody way.

Ross It is. But it turns out I made bad life choices.

Ellie The poverty thing?

Ross That, yeah.

Ellie It is a problem. Mind you, I still have it, and I didn't have your talent, so count yourself lucky.

Ross You had talent.

Ellie No I didn't. I had fun.

Ross I thought you were good. You sounded good yesterday.

Ellie No I didn't.

Ross Stop fishing.

Ellie I'm not. Not really.

Ross You totally are fishing.

Ellie You were good and Joe might have been, but that got complicated.

Ross Yeah.

Ellie Oh well.

Ross There is this moment that happens in young lives of total possibility, like you're a plant growing a metre a day, and it's actually with hindsight a very narrow window where you might get into some kind of creativity. I mean of course it is, life is short, childhood is shorter, but if you find a gear at the right age it's like a rocket. Anything could happen. You could turn into anyone.

Ellie You have to have the confidence to carry it off.

Ross And a lack of back-up plans.

Ellie And a lot of rigour.

Ross Yeah, that's true. Anyone who can really play, you know just from looking at their hands, their hands are different. Because they do it all the time. You need resilience. Because it all needs forcing into being, you know? And obviously you need to enjoy that, you need to find that fun. It takes a certain type of personality.

Ellie I was never serious about it. Actually I don't know if that's true. I think I was encouraged not to take it seriously. I think for women of my generation, I don't know what it's like now, but for me the whole thing was actually very male? It's ridiculous, but music seemed very male. And girls seemed to have a sort of secondary role. I think I could have been serious, but I fell into that, and now I do something different.

Ross Bit intense.

Ellie Is it?

Ross I didn't know we were doing Gender Studies.

Ellie I'm just sharing my experience.

Ross Fair enough.

Ellie You don't recognise it because you've always done the male genius act.

Ross The what?

Ellie You know exactly what I mean. Behaving badly because you deserved to. You know exactly what I mean.

Ross I never did it because I thought I was brilliant. I think it probably comes from shame.

Ellie Shut up.

Ross No, really. If you don't think you're any good at anything, you test yourself to try and prove yourself wrong. I think it was mostly that for me.

Ellie I think to be a singer you have to think you're better than other people.

Ross No way. It's the opposite. Or it is for me. And it's a novichok benefit, is it?

Ellie In theory.

Ross I think everyone's forgotten about it now. I was actually flying through Russia on the day it happened. I was on the way to Japan with my girlfriend, and we had to change on the way in Russia. And they swept us with a beeper, and my girlfriend set it off, and they took us into this side room in the airport and started asking questions. But we didn't speak Russian. And none of the guys there spoke any English. And I tell you, it was fucking intense. I was pretty scared, if I'm honest, we were both pretty scared, we wanted to cry. They'd taken our phones, and you're thinking, do I get a lawyer? But I probably don't because I'm not under arrest. But surely I at least get

a translator? Or then they'll arrest me and I'll be in
a Russian prison. And then this guy from our first flight just
sort of – barged in. He just forced his way into the room
and started translating. He was nothing to do with
anything, he was just a member of the public on our flight,
but he was Georgian, and he spoke Russian and English. So
he started translating for us all, and it turned out we'd set
off this radioactivity check. We'd shown up positive for
some kind of reading. So he said they need to search your
stuff, and we were like, cool, do whatever you like, we
haven't got anything so do whatever, thank God we hadn't
tried to carry any stash, and they searched our bags and
they searched us, not extreme like, not strip search, but they
searched us and then let us go. And this Georgian guy
wasn't even there to say thanks to. He'd caught his next
flight. We missed ours, we had to wait for the next one, but
they let us on, I guess to get us out of there. And then we
got off the plane in Japan, and there were pictures of actual
Salisbury on the TV. Like, I looked up in the arrivals lounge,
and there was film of the park that we used to get stoned in.
People in hazmats. Yellow tape. And the ticker at the
bottom of the screen wasn't in English. So I thought I was
in a fucking dream. I thought, no wonder we came up
radioactive, because I must be so high on something right
now. But yeah. I wasn't. And the weird thing is, here I am,
living proof, on the day of the Salisbury novichok hit, I was
scanned for radioactivity in an airport in Russia. I wasn't
living in Salisbury then. I hadn't even been here for years.
And they'd never have known that I had a connection. But
they did know I was a British national. So I wonder about
that. Whether they swiped everyone or whether they just
did people from the UK. I don't know how it works, spy
shit, what people plan for. But was I checked in case I was
a revenge attack?

Ellie That's not real.

Ross It is real. That all happened.

Ellie Shit.

Ross I know. That really happened.

Ellie I wasn't here but my mum was here through it. She was calling me every day.

Ross Why a door handle? I kept thinking that. I suppose you can be sure that everyone would touch it. But it's like a kid's prank isn't it. Like treacle in the lock. Why not a gun to the head or whatever?

Ellie I think everyone was luckier than they let on.

Ross Do you reckon?

Ellie I think they never made it public how close. I think it was Lizzie Gardens where they found it.

Ross Is that why the hazmats?

Ellie I think so, yeah. My mate ran a sort of boat hire company that went up the Avon, you booked him for an hour and he took people out on a punt, and he punted this couple up past Lizzie's and the willows were meant to be where they found it. Which was the spot where we used to get stoned. My mate said that looked like the place they were searching. Cos they'd fenced off the park but they hadn't fenced the river, so he went right past them with this couple on a first date on a punt.

Ross Hell of a first date.

Ellie Something to tell the grandkids. They buried the cars that got searched in the end. I think we were luckier than they let on. When it happened I realised I had Salisbury all wrong. I thought it was the middle of nowhere. I thought it was the back of beyond, like a left-behind England sort of thing. It's not. It's the centre. It's the English dreaming. It's where English people imagine they're from. That's why they came here. They attacked the collective unconscious.

Ross I suppose the one strange thing. I saw it on the TV. Out in Japan, they were showing Lizzie Gardens. And I looked at it, and I thought, that's me. That is my life, and where I'm from, and I'm not there now, but it was once a part of me, and so in a way it's always been a part of me. That is me. I recognised it on the telly. Buried under years. I never thought of it till then.

Enter Joe.

Ellie Hey! Are you all right?

Joe I'm sorry.

Ellie What happened?

Joe I wasn't going to come.

Ellie Why not? What's up?

Ross You all right, mate?

Joe I'm not sure we should do this.

Ellie What's the matter?

Joe I couldn't sleep last night. I think it's really stupid.

Ellie Why?

Joe It's selfish. It's self-indulgent. And I don't feel better, and I thought I would. If we wanted to do something about novichok we could just give some money.

Ross We don't have any money.

Joe No, but this isn't the way to fix that. This is just – it's sentimental. It's nostalgia.

Ellie Is that bad?

Joe It's a waste of everyone's time. This is me just needing to grow up.

Ross Right.

Ross stands up.

What's the time?

Ellie Twenty past ten.

Ross Okay. Here's what we're gonna do, all right? I'm gonna put my guitar away now, and we're gonna lock this hall and go out. And we're gonna have a fry-up, then we're gonna have a pint.

Ellie Are we?

Ross We will rehearse in the afternoon and evening. First we have to sort our heads out.

Joe No, but –

Ross This is also part of rehearsal. This is also part of being in a band. Joe, listen to me. I'm a professional musician. I know better than anyone else that yes, of course this stuff is self-indulgent. Of course it's nostalgic. It's people having fun. It's a completely stupid way to spend your life. That doesn't mean it doesn't make people happy. It doesn't mean we don't get people out their houses, and out of their lives for an evening, and give them an excuse to have a gin and keep their marriages going for a little while longer. You do that, and you also have fun. It is probably less helpful than building wells in Africa. That doesn't mean it's totally pointless. If you looked at everything like that, you couldn't live. So come on. We'll shake it off. Let's go to the pub.

Joe No, but, mate –

Ross I'm not listening, Joe. We're going to the pub.

2

*The hall again. Night. The band play a song. They're a bit
pissed. They finish with a flourish.*

Ross Cool!

Joe That sounded all right.

Ross Yeah, it did. That's cool.

Ellie Anyone want another drink?

Joe Go on.

Ellie goes to the kitchen.

Ross You know your trouble.

Joe What?

Ross You know your trouble.

Ellie enters with wine.

Ellie He hasn't got trouble.

Joe Yes I have.

Ross You need to get out of your head more.

Joe I am.

Ross What?

Joe I am out my head.

Ellie Have some more then.

Ross I don't mean pissed. I mean decompression.

Joe I know what you mean.

Ross No you don't.

Joe Yes I do.

Ross You don't, or you wouldn't be so tightly coiled. You need to find ways to relax.

Joe I am relaxed.

Ross Yeah, ways that aren't drinking.

Joe No way.

Ellie Don't listen to him, Joe. He's being mean.

Ross I'm not being mean! I'm trying to help him! You need to spend more time around people.

Joe That's what this was. That's what I'm trying to do.

Ross Well that's good then.

Joe I find it hard so I started small, yeah? I started with just you two, cos I remembered you. You know me. You know who I am. And you can remember me when I was normal.

Ellie You were never normal.

Joe I mean properly alive.

Ross Do you not feel alive any more?

Joe Not really. No, I don't, if I'm honest.

Ross Why not?

Joe I dunno. I left it behind.

Ross Where?

Joe I guess. When I was married.

Ellie Yeah.

Joe After she got ill. I wasn't all right. But I didn't know how to tell anyone.

Ross What happened?

Ellie Ross!

Ross If you wanna talk about it.

Joe She took a pill and her words went. Just like that. She screamed and screamed. She didn't know me when she next saw me. I couldn't find her for the first few days. I was away in Wales when she got ill. In the end I found her on the Isle of Wight. She'd caught a ferry. They put her in the hospital, found my number in her phone. I don't know why she was out there. We never went there before, when she was well. At first I thought she'd just get better. She used to get ill sometimes, she took life too hard. Sometimes she'd break down. Appendicitis, gastritis. But a week passed and she still hadn't spoken. I waited for her. I spent all my money on this B&B, and it's so stupid, isn't it, having to worry about something like money at a time like that. There ought to be a fund for when these things happen. So people with their loved ones don't run out of cash. After two weeks they said they'd get her off the island, and I thought that meant they'd send her home. But that wasn't it. There was a bed on the mainland. They said it was gonna be a long-term thing. So they moved her and put her under section. And I'd go and see her every day. Get the train from our flat cos I didn't have a car, and go and visit through visiting hours. I never missed a day. She was there five months. After a while we were allowed into town at weekends when I visited, a few hours at a time. Little by little she built back up like that. One little thing after another. When she came out she was a different person. She wasn't better. She had night terrors. I just held her. Tried to hold her. Over time she got herself together. I spent all my money on this private place as well. Private sort of rehab, when she came out. We could only afford a few weeks, but anything at all to get her better. I just wanted her back, you know? You fall in love with someone and then they disappear. I just wanted my wife like before. But that never happened. Never saw her again. After the pill she was a different person. Her job let her go and she wanted a career change. Said she needed something that could better support her, because she was different now, she was fragile. She looked for it for a year or so. I supported both of us and she job hunted. And then she found one. And then she was gone. I let her have the flat. She was ill now, she was fragile. I could always start again. I let her have the flat and I slept in my car for the first little while, my last act of love, her being comfortable and me like that, till I got somewhere I could rent. It was too hard for me at first, really. All the logistics. I think I just wanted to curl up and go. But then I chose not to. I got a little flat. I don't know how she pays her bills. I guess she got a lodger. Or maybe she's seeing someone else. I keep out the way of her. When I see her it triggers something. Makes me want my old life back. I can't have that. It doesn't exist now. I pay my rent and I go to work and I hope one day that I'll feel different. I hope I'll get back to wanting to be happy. Knowing how to be happy. Knowing how to live.

Ellie Fuck.

Ross Mate.

Joe What?

Ellie That's incredibly rubbish.

Joe Yeah. But everyone has something.

Ellie Yeah. But that is incredibly rubbish.

Joe Thank you.

Ellie I'm sorry.

Joe Thank you.

Ross Mate.

Joe You see how I got to this then, don't you?

Ellie Got to what?

Joe To doing this. I thought, if I could just do something that used to make me happy. Then maybe I could be a person again. This is stupid, yeah. But after she'd left me. I'm talking too much, aren't I. After I was on my own. I kept going back and back into the past. I suppose because it was comforting or something? I suppose before things felt like they'd gone wrong. Sometimes it feels like getting the bends to go through the years of your life, you know? While I was looking after her, I didn't see anyone else, didn't do anything else, that's what I was, I looked after her and that was my meaning. So then not to have that meaning any more. I wanted other stories of myself. And I changed my job to do that, and I got my flat, but I also went backwards, sort of looking, sort of thing. I had this dream. Maybe it came from playing little model men. I dreamed of asking you both to come back and see me, and help me out of this sort of. I dunno. This basement I couldn't get myself out of. And I know we missed the moment really. We should have done it in 2020 or 2021, or it was your fault in '22 when you were an anti-vaxxer.

Ross I wasn't –

Joe No, but you know what I mean. But I'm glad we're doing it. As long as it's not selfish.

Ellie Of course it isn't.

Joe A bit maybe.

Ellie No it isn't.

Joe I'm glad we're doing it all the same. I don't think we can rehearse any more though. I can't really see my hands.

Ellie That's okay. It's bedtime maybe.

Joe Can you guys get home?

Ellie We'll be fine.

Ross I'll get a taxi.

Ellie There, see? We're fine.

Joe I can walk home.

Ellie Will you be okay?

Joe I walk round Salisbury drunk all the time. What would have happened if you hadn't got together?

Ellie Sorry?

Joe If we'd stayed together. Would we still be a band?

Ellie I don't think I was ever that serious.

Joe I think about it. If I hadn't seen you both getting off that train.

Ellie Maybe not tonight, Joe, while we're emotional.

Joe You must think about it. Do you wish it hadn't happened?

Ross Why?

Joe Because it was a shit thing to do.

Ross You guys had broken up.

Joe No we hadn't.

Ellie Yes we had, Joe.

Joe Like a day earlier.

Ross You guys had broken up. We got together.

Ellie And now we're three old friends.

Ross There was nothing to regret, Joe.

Joe We might have got back together.

Ellie No, we wouldn't.

Joe Why not?

Ellie It was over. I was going away to uni.

Joe And I wasn't? Is that what it was?

Ellie No, it wasn't about that. I just meant I was going to be far away.

Joe So was he. You slept with him.

Ellie It was never a serious thing.

Ross Thanks.

Ellie Well, sorry. I think you know that though.

Joe We could have had that last summer together.

Ellie I think we'd outgrown each other.

Joe But you hadn't outgrown him.

Ellie Joe, shut up, you'll regret this in the morning.

Joe Sorry. I'm sorry. I just didn't understand. I loved you. Both of you. I loved this, you know? And we sat round the radio on results day and they played our song on Radio 2. And nothing's ever been that good again. And then our parents saying we shouldn't. Saying it was time to grow up now. And then you said that you were leaving. And then I saw you both get off the train. And he kissed you, and you took his hand.

Ross All I knew was that you had broken up.

Joe Like a day earlier.

Ellie More like a fortnight.

Joe And that makes it all right?

Ross We were kids, and kids behave badly. I'm sorry if your feelings were hurt.

Joe What kind of fucking apology is that? You both got to have lives. I got left here.

Ross Yours was a life too. You just haven't liked it.

Ellie Let's call cabs.

Joe I'm sorry.

Ross It's all right.

Joe Ellie, I'm sorry.

Ellie It's just the booze talking.

Joe Don't ghost me.

Ellie We won't. We'll be here tomorrow morning.

Ross Might be better if we push it back to lunch.

Joe Don't ghost me.

Joe exits.

Ross What the fuck was all that?

Ellie He's drunk. Forget it. He will in the morning.

Ross There was nothing shady about us.

Ellie I know.

Ross Do you not think?

Ellie I dunno. It was a bit quick.

Ross You guys were over.

Ellie It was quick.

Ross You were over. I didn't know we were just a fling.

Ellie I was just playing it down.

Ross You could have said if that was how you felt.

Ellie I was just playing it down because we're all pissed and now is not the time.

Ross Do you think I came back to play some village hall gig? Ellie, I came back to see you again.

Ellie Well you did the wrong thing then. That was a lifetime ago, Ross.

Ross I didn't say that. I didn't say I thought we'd get back together. I just wanted to see you again. I didn't know we were just a summer thing.

Ellie Well we weren't, were we. But he doesn't need to know that. He doesn't need to know why it didn't work out.

Ross If we'd kept her.

Ellie We were too young.

Ross But if we had.

Ellie Then our lives would be different.

Ross Do you think about it?

Ellie All the time. I'm going through fucking IVF, Ross, my partner and I are struggling to conceive. So yes. I think about it. All the time.

Ross Me too.

Ellie Well then.

Ross I wish we'd gone for it.

Ellie Do you?

Ross I don't know. Sometimes, yeah.

Ellie I've thought that sometimes. From time to time.

Ross So don't say it wasn't a serious thing.

Ellie He doesn't ever need to know this, Ross. This is something private that's just between us.

Ross What about your partner?

Ellie I haven't told him.

Ross Why not?

Ellie I didn't want to go back.

Ross But you came here though.

Ellie I didn't think we'd say all this. I was just gonna have a nice weekend.

Ross Have we not?

Ellie I didn't want to talk about this.

Ross But surely this is why you came.

Ellie I don't know. He was fucking persistent.

Ross Yeah.

Ellie I couldn't explain it to him. Please can we just go home? I'm tired now. I want to sleep and start again tomorrow morning.

Ross You shouldn't be drinking if you're having IVF.

Ellie I know. I fucking know, all right?

Ross So what's going on?

Ellie I'm not sure about my life! Is that okay? Isn't everyone like that? I'm not sure that I'm doing the right things. And sometimes that makes me behave erratically. Tonight, that seems to have made me drink.

Ross You'd be a good mum.

Ellie Oh.

Ross I think. From what I know of you.

Ellie I just don't know if I want to be one. But you run out of time too quick, so I'm trying.

Ross I'm sorry I brought it all up again.

Ellie It's okay. Might be better though if we just leave it.

Ross I can see that.

The sound of a car outside.

Ellie That's my cab, I think.

Ross All right. I'll lock up. You go.

Ellie All right. Night then.

Ross Yeah. Night.

Ellie exits. Ross sits down and plays a song.

3

The next day. Ross is already onstage; Joe enters.

Ross Sore head?

Joe Little bit.

Ross Good sign.

Joe Is it?

Ross Sign of a night well spent.

Joe How was yours?

Ross Yeah, all right.

Joe Did you and Ellie –

Ross No, mate. That was a lifetime ago.

Joe Seems more recent than that to me. I guess I've had less life since.

Ross Twenty-four hours in everyone's day.

Joe Maybe.

Ross Well there are.

Joe But some people fill it better.

Ross Honestly, Joe, that was so long ago. I never think of it now. Is that why we did this?

Joe What?

Ross Me and Ellie.

Joe I guess in a way, yeah.

Ross Unfinished business.

Joe I just wanted to see you guys again.

Ross I feel like we won't hang out any more after this, though. We might say we will. But our lives don't cross over.

Joe Maybe it's more like a saying goodbye thing.

Ross We did that.

Joe But don't you think a lot of things still felt held open? It's so arbitrary, falling apart because of the school year. Not because of us. I thought there was so much left hanging.

Ross Maybe.

Joe Right?

Ross Last night, me and Ellie. After you left, we had this conversation – I dunno. I can't talk about it. That's why I said yes.

Joe To see her? I thought so. You'd never have said yes just to me.

Ross I dunno, mate.

Joe But you came back to see her.

Ross Did you ask her first?

Joe Yeah.

Ross You were the same then.

Joe Or I just knew you wouldn't say yes without her.

Ross You weren't still together. When we got together.
Don't remember it like that cos it isn't what happened. You
make it into less than it was when you do that.

Joe I probably get to choose how I remember my own life.

Ross But I'm telling you you're an unreliable witness.

Joe And I'm telling you that I'll never forgive you.

Ross You'd broken up.

Joe I'll still never forgive you.

Ellie enters.

Ellie Sorry.

Ross You're okay.

Ellie Yeah, fine. What's the plan?

Joe One last play through, then we open the house.

Ellie Sounds good. You guys okay?

Ross Yeah, fine.

Joe It feels like none of us wants to be here.

Ellie No, you're okay. Pre-match nerves. Come on, let's
warm up.

Joe I got us something.

Ellie What?

Joe Hang on.

*Joe goes to his bag. He takes out a T-shirt and holds it
out. It says 'The Band Back Together'.*

Ellie Really?

Joe We never liked our name.

Ellie But that's not a good band name.

Joe It sort of is though. It's what everyone wishes would happen.

Ross And you want us to wear that?

Joe Good brand identity.

Ross Yeah?

Joe It's important.

Ross Why do we need branding? We're never going to do this again.

Joe We might.

Ellie I do think it's a good name, actually.

Joe Thank you.

Ellie I'll wear it.

Joe Yeah?

Ellie Give it here.

Joe chucks Ellie a T-shirt.

Joe Ross?

Ross Yeah, all right.

Joe chucks Ross another T-shirt.

Ellie You should have got different colours.

Joe Why?

Ellie So we didn't all match.

Joe I wanted us to match.

Ellie Okay.

Joe Is that a problem?

Ellie No, I suppose not.

Joe You think it looks stupid.

Ellie No, it's great. I might just go and –

Joe Yeah.

Ellie exits to change.

Ross Not because we might do this again. Because we won't.

Joe Yeah. I get it.

Ross and Joe change into the T-shirt.

Ross There you go.

Joe Because we won't.

Ross Sorry, mate. Too long ago for me.

Joe I know.

Ross How are you feeling?

Joe Yeah, nervous. I don't know whether we'll be any good.

Ross That's the fun isn't it.

Joe I mean I suppose so. Might be more fun to know you were great.

Enter Ellie.

Ellie Looks like sports stash.

Ross No, it looks good.

Ellie At least they'll know who's in the band.

Joe Exactly.

Ross They'd have known anyway.

Ellie Cos only the beautiful people are in the band?

Ross No, cos all of the audience are eighty.

Joe We don't know yet. Wait till the house opens.

Ellie Maybe no one's gonna come.

Ross We'll see.

Ellie If they don't it doesn't matter. We'll still do it. We'll have fun. And that's not nothing.

Joe Yeah.

Ellie Thank you for this, Joe.

Joe I didn't do anything.

Ellie No, you made it happen. Has it helped?

Joe Erm. I don't know. I feel quite iceberg.

Ellie What do you mean?

Joe Like I've broken off of where I was, and I'm drifting. I feel quite like I can't get home.

Ellie I'm sorry, mate.

Joe It's all right. It's not your fault. I just thought this would make me feel better.

Ellie I feel better, if that helps.

Joe Do you?

Ellie Yeah. I feel really grateful. Ross, can I tell him?

Ross What?

Ellie Can I *tell* him?

Ross Oh. Okay. If you want to.

Ellie Thank you.

She turns to Joe and takes a deep breath.

Ross and me got pregnant back then. I'm sorry we never told you. We didn't keep her, obviously. And it's right we didn't. It's fucking heartbreaking but it's right we didn't. But after that decision we never talked again. I mean, not completely, but more or less, right?

Ross Yeah. More or less.

Ellie For obvious reasons. And I nearly didn't do this, for the same reasons. But I'm glad I have. And I'm grateful to you. Because I've felt ashamed of this huge bit of my life for a long time. And I don't want to feel that any more. We did our best. That's the story. Long ago, in a different time, some kids did the best they could, and it hurt. I'd love not to feel shame about that any more. So I'm glad I'm here cos it's like coming out of hiding.

Joe I didn't know about this.

Ellie No one did, no. (*To Ross.*) You okay?

Ross Yeah.

Ellie Come on then, you two. Pick up your instruments.

Ross Do you want five, or –

Ellie I'm fine. I'm really okay. Come on, let's get on with it.

They get their instruments.

We might never have done this again. I'm glad we have.

Joe Yeah.

Ellie You guys okay?

Ross Yeah, fine.

Ellie All right then. One, two, three, four –

They play a final song.
Lights.
End.

Hidden Track

A STRANGER COMES TO TOWN

Author's Note

Because *The Band Back Together* is a play about music, this playtext seemed a little like putting out an album. Thinking about the book like that was beguiling – a lot of memories came back of life as a teenager, the bands I was in and the dreams we all shared. One thing that came back very strongly was that when I was a kid, I really liked hidden tracks: the recorded equivalent of an encore. I loved the sense they left behind of a larger world beyond the album I'd just listened to. It occurred to me that if I was going to do justice to the bands that blushed unseen down in Wiltshire at the start of this millennium and gave rise to *The Band Back Together*, I should put a hidden track in here.

Over the winter before making *The Band Back Together*, I travelled to the Isle of Mull to tell a story. I'd first visited the island in March 2023, and returned in November to make a show called *A Stranger Comes to Town* for An Tobar and Mull Theatre, which they toured over the course of that winter. In some ways it's a palimpsest of *The Band Back Together*, taking a radically different path through the same forest of emotions. And it's another show I made to tour village halls, part of a year of work dedicated to telling stories to particular communities. As a result of these synchronicities, the idea came to me of including it here as my hidden track.

A Stranger Comes to Town was first performed at Dervaig Hall on the Isle of Mull on 10 November 2023.

Writer and Performer Barney Norris
Composer Ailie Robertson
Stage Manager Louise Gregory

The audience enters an exploded shed, a construction made of reclaimed pallets, old corrugated iron, plastic sheeting, driftwood. Displayed on the walls of the shed and within the space are the wreckage and detritus of a life; and, more specifically, of time spent by the sea. Everything in this space is resonant with the memory of the sound of the sea. There is a deer skull on one wall; a storm lantern hanging above the set; a stack of old hardbacks, maybe an old encyclopedia; a small cairn of stones. There are maps and texts stuck to the walls. In the corner of the room, bottles filled with sea water, a stack of rice paper and a pile of pencils.

Projected images appear during the course of the show: images of Mull, of the sea, of forgetting. Images of old maps and old photos.

The text is like a story that is rotting back down and coming apart. Like something that's been washed over for several years already by the sea. I think of those drowned villages, where they say the tide still rings the church bells underwater.

An answerphone machine on a crate in the middle of the room is beeping. The play begins with someone from the audience playing the message, which prompts the following text to play, both through the handset and through the wider sound design:

I came to the sea, to Calgary. I walked out into cold blue water. Hoping to unravel. To release all pain.

I looked back at the hills, the woods. This must be how the seals see us, queuing for our ice creams. We must look so hemmed in on the shore there. They can watch us and just swim away. Where I come from there are people who believe the dead come back sometimes, as selkies. Human spirits in the bodies of a seal. And they haunt the shorelines they called home, and you can still reach them, still hear them singing.

I don't believe there are ghosts in the world. I think the ghosts are inside us. After a loved one dies, there is memory. That's all that matters. And one or two knick-knacks to remind you.

I have kept all the books she bought me. And I've kept a skull we found on Mull. We were eating fish and chips in a car park with an abandoned building at the edge. Some old store house for the big house nearby. No doors on it any more, rain lashed, some broken pieces of pottery lying around. We went to explore. There were old clay jugs stored in a crate. There was broken glass from old medicine bottles. There were floor tiles an inch thick. It was like someone had just finished clearing a nineteenth-century house, then gone for a walk, and the next people to turn up had been us. We walked round the back of the building, and there we found a deer skull lying on the ground. Almost stripped of flesh. We picked it up. We put it in the back of the car. We drove it home, the length of Mull, the ferry to Oban, all of Scotland, the length of England. It hangs on the wall now. A piece of the wild we took with us. And what does that say about us, I wonder?

What she noticed about Mull was the redness. In bracken and soil and venison, everywhere redness taken from the clay.

What I noticed was everything abandoned. Bone and clay jug, glass and plastic, old stone houses with the doors knocked off. Tiles and chip paper. Stone coughed out by the earth. A map of the shipwrecks crowding round the island. Hundreds of timber structures rotting down, under the water, homes for the selkies. An ancient church that stood on the site of an ancient church where someone told me a man was buried alive beneath the altar.

On Iona, in the driving rain, we climbed a little staircase to a small cell room by the west door, the entrance barely wider than my body. Above our heads, moss and lichen were working to take the whole structure apart again. Like the deer skull rotting down. I noticed all wreckages are actually relics. All relics are actually wreckage. If you wait long enough, there's no difference between a thing that's been salvaged and saved, and a thing abandoned, left behind.

Or can you tell whether there was once love here? When you stand in Calgary bay and look back at the shoreline, can you tell how much this place mattered?

Film images start to play over this next section.

Three miles east of the prison gates there was a drab and lonely beach subsisting in the lee of a hill. The broken-off end of Northern Ireland. I left the car and walked to the water's edge. Stripped down. The water was really too cold to swim, but it felt like a baptism to walk out, immerse myself, hope I'd never set foot in Magilligan again.

Not that it was the worst of prisons. An old ex-army place, all the barracks huts had been converted into workshops. You could learn bricklaying in one, carpentry in another. Electrics. Reading. Plumbing. Things like that. And there was a prison marathon every year, running back and forth till you'd done twenty-six miles. I walked into the sea and left it all behind. And when I got out, that was when the call came.

I caught the ferry back that night. I stayed in the concourse on my own. Went and looked out over the sides. Watched a man so drunk he decided he had to undress because he was overheating. A huge man, he stripped out of his shirt but left his tie round his neck and lay on the seats, gasping for air. Like a seal lying there in the concourse.

I came into Holyhead early in the morning. Just about to start getting light. This was where they arrested him.

I'd been here before myself. Spent a week between one Christmas and New Year walking this coastline, walking towards my father, in a way. Starting up here at Holyhead then following the coast round as far as Criccieth, where my father told me once he went on childhood holidays. Then walking inland to Ffestiniog, where my family came from. The slate mountains we had to leave a hundred years ago because we were starving.

I used to do a lot of that, walking the coastlines. Walking back to childhood a lot of the time, haunting old places. I remember walking out from Exmouth, following the river, looking for beaches where I'd been young. Then pitching my tent on the cliffs above Salcombe and sleeping better than I'd ever slept before, and waking at dawn to open the tent and crawl out into the morning, only to find a young deer lying in front of me, sleeping in what it must have thought was shelter from the wind. It woke, and leapt, and ran.

Why did I go to the sea back then? What do people look for when they travel to the coast? Rest and relaxation, yes; and a feeling of smallness maybe, a feeling of awe at the sea's indifference. There's a kind of forgiveness, maybe, in the sea. Whatever you've failed at. Whoever you've let down, you're so small, really, when you set the weight of your life against the ocean. So how can your pain be as big as it feels? Or the pain you caused to other people.

The sea is forgiveness. A place to release trouble. Let go, let everything that hurt you fall away. And be in your body. Feel the water and the sun on your skin and remember this nest of thoughts, fears, regrets, it's not real. It's inside you.

You could let it fall away. You could fill a bottle with sea water, and pour your pain in there. And the sea would forget it for you. It forgets everything.

On the night ferry I met a man who told me his job while he was still working was to monitor the quality of butter in Ireland. He told me the reason Kerrygold was called Kerrygold was that it was the only county that didn't make butter, so couldn't gain a competitive advantage. Thinking back, I think he might have been lying. He said he caught the ferry most days because he spent his retirement attending trials in the public galleries of Dublin and Liverpool. Different trials on different days. I asked if there'd been a big trial he'd been involved with. He said there wasn't. He'd done jury duty once. A pretty straightforward case of theft. I suppose all of us end up haunting somewhere, so why not a courtroom? In the end he got bored of me, got up and left. I went back to staring out over the side, at the waves, at the night, at the endless forgetting.

At Holyhead I drove off the ferry and back through the starving slate mountains, towards a life where no one was waiting.

A skull on the wall and the memory of love.

Lights focus on the deer skull. The film turns off. Out of the deer skull on the far wall, the voice continues.

She told me she'd be all right for a week, so I flew to Cape Town. They met me at the airport. A nondescript rental car. Driving down Nelson Mandela Way they told me scare stories. How people dropped bricks off the bridges at night to stop cars so they could rob them. How people who'd stopped by this roadside with punctures or overheated engines had been kidnapped or killed. I didn't believe them. I looked out the windows at the townships, and felt moved by the ingenuity of the people there, who'd built homes out of wooden pallets, discarded corrugated iron, plastic sheeting. This stuff other people had thrown away, turned into shelter, a kind of home. The driver said most people living in the townships had good homes in the villages inland, and only came to Cape Town for the work. I thought, believe what you want, mate. People, given any reasonable opportunity, will look away.

I wondered whether it was wrong of me to find the townships beautiful. The resilience, the defiance. Cobbling a life out of odds and ends the way all of us feel as if we do, but never like this, never adversity like this. Washed up on the shores of an indifferent city, finding no welcome there, no security, gathering flotsam washed up with them and lashing it together to keep themselves safe. The real heroes of our age are here. People finding ways to live. Having just got off the plane from England, I felt damned by my connection to them. The way their poverty and my wealth were part of the same thing, the same rigged system.

When I think of lawyers shuttling between South Africa and Northern Ireland, I think of the nineties, when the same people who'd run the Truth and Reconciliation Commission decamped to Belfast to oversee the peace process. I try to imagine the optimism of that moment. I wonder whether we're still capable of it, in these days that feel like last days, standing in the wreckage of our world, our civilisation. Here I am preparing an appeal for a man convicted of people smuggling. I suppose I'm part of the same thing those other lawyers were doing. But it doesn't feel that way sometimes.

I try to let it all go. Try not to think. Focus on the next thing. Get through the day.

After the meeting I walk down to the sea, the fresh of the spray where it's crashing on rocks, the intoxicating brightness of the air. The light is different here. Blue, crystalline. I am so far away from her and I want to go home. I try to concentrate on my breathing. Slow and even till I've let everything go. I watch the water flung up into the air every time it breaks against the rocks. I imagine I'm not here, in this life, researching this case, listening to these stories of harm and indifference.

The storm lantern above the set starts to flash, the film plays again, and the following text emerges from the lantern.

We drove back from Iona in steady rain, hearts in mouths on the single-track roads, scanning the rock falls to try and make out which ones were recent. We came to a pair of hairpin bends up a hill so steep the only way I could think to get up was to put the car in second and floor the accelerator, praying we didn't meet anything coming down. At the top, we stopped to let out heart rates drop by a stone cairn. There were plaques screwed into a small tor nearby. We climbed up to them. They commemorated drivers, strangers who'd passed through there. It wasn't clear whether they'd all died on those corners. Surely the locals wouldn't have stood for it? Letting the ghosts pile up that way. We climbed back down the soft grass of the hill, and got back in the car, and drove on. Part of the trip was about trying to see whales, dolphins. We kept our eyes on the sea to our left as we travelled as much as we could, but saw nothing. The whole trip, we didn't see a whale or a dolphin. But several seals, a porpoise leaping, a female capercaillie, and, by the Tobermory lighthouse, a nuclear submarine coming up for air at nightfall. Sitting silent and sleek in the water while the people in the holiday cottage by the lighthouse knew nothing about it and got on with dinner.

A few miles on from the stone cairn, we came to a signpost for an art gallery and pulled in. The gallery was a small tin shed with a Perspex roof that let in the light; inside it were several small ceramic replicas of South African township buildings. In all their salvaged, cobbled-together beauty.

Reproduced now as works of art, in a tin shed on Mull, miles from the next building. The woman who ran the gallery and made the work spoke of her unease making art from those structures. Whether it could ever be right to draw attention to the beauty of them, the creativity behind them, the love and the hope. I said I thought that was all in the work she'd made. I was transfixed by them because I wasn't sure whether they were a tribute, or a rebuke.

Another phone starts to ring. Film continues. When someone answers the phone, the text begins again.

She'd grown up inland the same as I did, but every chance she got she'd go down to West Wittering, Mudeford, Bournemouth, or further west into Cornwall and the emptier beaches there. Sometimes to swim, but mostly just to listen, lie on the beach and hear the sea's breathing.

I started to wonder whether there was something draining for the people who lived by the sea all the time about people like us, who came and went. When we left, did we take something away? Were we stripping their landscape?

When I've lived in coastal towns, I've seen how much those places need visitors. But what is the cost of all that trade, all those people coming and going? Does it feel like loss, again and again?

And the image comes to me of four-by-fours departing, crunch of gravel, and tinkling, bright-lit, empty arcades.

When you live by the sea, do you come to hate the visitors, at the same time as relying on them? Or is it wonderful to feel so wealthy, to live in the midst of something so many people need?

I think I come to the sea so I can hear things. There's a kind of deafness inland. And I need sometimes to leave behind the palaces and temples we've constructed, tomorrow's ruins, tomorrow's archaeological digs, and recognise all that I've done with my life as relic and wreckage, something I'll one day leave behind, a palimpsest of who I was but no more than that. And try to step out of all that noise, and simply sit and realise I'm alive. Sit and listen to my breathing. Know that the rest is time coming and going. The rest is a substance in which we drown, that doesn't matter to the ocean, which is going to forget everything.

Out of a creel net, the text continues.

When I think about what they went through. All the rich panoply of each of their lives reduced down into the dark container, all the wealth and variety of who they were hemmed into that one journey overland to Tunisia, into the container, round Spain and Portugal, into Holyhead docks, the claustrophobia overwhelms me. And I turn to my things and put my hand on the table near to me, and feel the grained texture of its surface. I put my hand on the chair where I'm sitting. I look at the space my life takes up. The things I have room and security enough to surround myself with. A skull on the wall. The things I've never been obliged to leave behind so I can fit into some small space. And I recognise my wealth. But at the same time these things become so beautiful to me.

I used to think there was an ugliness to it, a kind of consumerism to furniture, artworks, books, white goods, house plants, crockery, cutlery, glassware. Having and acquiring and gathering and owning, a fetish for possession, a fetish for money. But when I think of the air in that container. And stripping your life down so you'd fit in that container. Then the things I own and everyone owns become a kind of celebration, also. This detritus and flotsam and driftwood we have gathered is a sign we don't have to leave tonight. It's a sign we don't have to carry all we own. Splay it out. Lay it all out round you and count your blessings.

May everyone own too much, and sometimes dust it. May everyone on earth have that right.

In a different part of the set, another phone rings.

He told me he drove trucks for a living, and he met a man who wanted trucks loaded onto ships at port cities. These were vehicles no longer in good enough condition for European legislation, being sold into Africa to be refitted and used there for a few years longer. The same way old London cabs get sent to Bristol. The man he met had lived in England all his life, but his grandparents had come over from Ireland. He said his grandfather used to catch rats for a living, and his grandmother sold pegs door to door. Now the man owned half the houses in his town.

He said it was the construction of the M25 that did it. Instead of just advertising in the Yellow Pages nearby to his home, he placed ads in every phone book distributed around the London Orbital. Watford, Hemel, St Albans, Potters Bar, Epping, Brentwood, Romford, Grays, Tilbury, Dartford, Orpington, Caterham, Redhill, Epsom, Weybridge, Woking, Slough, dozens of others. A quarter of a million quid in adverts in the late 1980s. Ads for glazing, tiling, bricklaying, skip hire, construction, demolition. He made a fortune. And some years later he got into selling old lorries to Africa.

The only problem was that ports had a quota; any one outfit could only load so many vehicles onto a container ship at any one place and time. My client's job, as he told it to me, was to drive lorries out to every port in England, as the container ships went round. He'd load on a lorry at Liverpool, Holyhead, Cardiff, Plymouth, Southampton, Portsmouth, Tilbury maybe, catching the train back home each time. Till there were half a dozen lorries on the one ship that had all been driven on by him. And either no one noticed, or more likely no one mentioned. That, my client told me, was all the dealings he'd had with this man. And he had no associates in Cape Town or anywhere else in Africa. So he couldn't have known about his other business.

I went to each port, spoke to officials at the docks there. Each time hating leaving her. Trying to understand the scam.

In every place I visited, the same bars and takeaways, the same signs and traffic, the same slate-grey indifferent ocean staring in beneath the rain. I wondered what it must have been like for him. Driving different roads each time, only to arrive in the same place, load the same lorry onto the same ship, drink the same pint, catch the same train home.

In a different part of the set, the text continues.

In her hospital. The island of the hospital. High above the city, a ship at sea. Experiencing sunsets at different times because from the third floor you looked down to the horizon. Watching the sun dip while in the streets around, cars were already driving with their lights on. We remembered an optical illusion we'd see sometimes from the cliffs near Brighton, where passing ships would seem to fly, because of the way the light caught the ocean. That was how we felt, up on the third floor. Our *Flying Dutchman*, unable to go home, trapped in the rigging high up above the city. Watching the whole world below us contort in currents that wore everything down, watching the buildings fade into driftwood.

Sometimes we'd look out and imagine it deserted. The buildings abandoned and transfigured into ruins. The roofs caving in, walls falling down. Oaks tearing up through the pavement beneath us. The water rising till it washed over everything. Flooding everything and sweeping us home.

I wished I could have taken her to the sea then. So she could fall back in the water and let go of her pain. A nice dream. But it offered no comfort. So I loved her there in the storm-lashed silence, on our *Flying Dutchman*, as the sun set.

I don't know whether I'll ever look at that hospital again. A piece of the wreckage of us, one of our relics. I wouldn't choose to, but if one day I drove by. If the satnav took me past it. Would I be able to tell there'd been love there? Would that be somehow written into the concrete?

Whatever remains beautiful in the remnants of old ruins is what looks to me like the memory of love. The mortar that once held stones together, the slate cut for rooftops, filigrees carved in stone. All of this was work worth doing for someone. A part of their lives was given to making that building. After the house falls, traces of that remain, in the well-cut stone, as the moss grows over and drags it back underground. You still see it. After the clearances, the crofters were remembered by the landscape they left, by the tumbled stone. Someone once cared about this place. A human life happened here. They felt what you're feeling.

Would I see all that written in her hospital? Or would I only see pain?

From the bottles, the text continues.

What I came here looking for is what we loved together. The memories I would choose to carry with me through the years that still remain. So I took a leave of absence, leaving behind my research for the appeal, driving back to her, to Oban, to Calgary again.

There had been a sighting a few days earlier of a minke whale. What she wanted to see most of all was orcas. They terrified me, but she loved them. She'd learned all the identifying features of the orcas whose pods passed near to these islands. And she never saw them. So I'll try to find them for her. I'll start here, then go on to Orkney. This is the best time of year to go. All the time I'm travelling, I will inscribe the memory of these places we shared into the mind's eye, the happiness we found here, not the pain that came later. I'll gather the lakes and red bracken and churches, the hawks and wild garlic, the streams and the waterfalls, brightly coloured houses, broken stones, wind-hobbled old woods, the red deer grazing, gather the forgiveness and forgetting of the sea. The clock in the harbour commemorating Isabella Bird. She saw this. We shared it. We had this much together.

All my life I've gone to the sea and left things behind me when I came home. My worries, my pain. Now I want to take something away. Not shells. Not driftwood. Not photographs or pebbles. Just the feeling of time by the ocean. The memory of the sound of the sea.

In the corner of the room you'll find glass bottles, and a stack of paper, and a pile of pencils. If you want to leave anything of your own behind when you leave this place. Anything you don't want to carry any more. Write it down on the paper, put it in the bottles. It will dissolve when it touches the water. It will be gone. If there's something you're tired of carrying with you, some loss, some stress, some failed ambition, why not leave that weight behind when you leave this room and turn for home?

Think about it. What you'd write. What would you let go of? What's holding you down? You've heard mine. All of it unravelled and gone. What part of your own life would you like to lose at sea?

The film turns off and the lights focus on the bottles.